THE ALLURE
OF PERMANENCE

ELDORADO STONE

A HEADWATERS COMPANY

First Edition

ISBN: 978-0-615-18661-0

Text by Michael Fraser, David Conover and Brent Spann

Designed by:

www.studioconover.com

Printed in the United States of America

Cover photo: The Cortile Collection, Plan One: The Bridges at Ranch Santa Fe

Lennar Communities

Bassenian/Lagoni Architects

Photo by Eric Figge

Stone profile on cover: Orchard Cypress Ridge with an overgrout technique

This book is dedicated to all the Developers, Architects,
Builders, Specifiers, Masons and Craftsmen whose vision
afforded the opportunity for Eldorado Stone. A special
dedication to all Eldorado Stone employees — past and
present — whose continued hard work and pioneering
efforts remain our inspiration to this day.

CONTENTS

Stone is remarkably full of life. It has character and personality. It communicates. Stone, in many ways, is a reflection of ourselves. Each one unique, none exactly alike, but all worthy of our admiration. It may be the reason why so many of us are drawn to its presence and so comfortable in its surroundings.

A home built with stone. It catches your eye and invites you in. Somehow, the furniture in a stone home just looks more comfy. The decorative touches more authentic. The lighting more romantic. But beyond its surface texture and contours hides its mystique. Somehow, those unique spaces dressed with stone help capture some of life's most memorable moments.

Remember that wine cellar where you tasted your first great Pinot Noir? Or, the gathering around the river rock fireplace, recalling memories recounted time and again with family and friends? And don't forget that stone front porch where you shared your first goodnight kiss.

There is stone in your past. And, hopefully, there is stone in your future. When you build with stone you rekindle those moments in life that are so treasured.

This book is a photographic homage to architectural stone. It's meant to take you on a visual journey through some of the finest homes graced with stone. And it's meant to be a source of inspiration when you decide to build with architectural stone veneer. Enjoy the stroll.

EXTERIORS

*" Every block of stone has a statue
inside it and it is the task of the
sculptor to discover it."*

–Michelangelo

Stone gives you options: The type of stone.
Its palette. How it is cut. How it is mortared.
Whether it is combined with other types of stone
or, perhaps, brick. As you'll see in this section,
the design possibilities are intriguing — and limitless.

Stone is powerful and stone is subtle. Stone can be the focal
point of a space, or it can simply complement other design
elements. A stone façade can be elegant or it can be rustic. It can
capture the feel of a chateau in the Loire Valley or a farmhouse
in the Pyrenees. And it can be completely modern.

In an artistic sense, stone is neither canvas nor brush; it is the
paint itself. Working together, a talented designer and a skilled
mason can create virtually any effect. Friendly, imposing, cozy,
inviting, dramatic, opulent, rustic, elegant — they're all possible
with stone.

Stone is also ever-changing. It's never boring. A stone
façade at dawn looks completely different at midday. And come
evening, a stone entrance graced by the light of the front porch
welcomes you home.

Stone can be an integral component for any architectural style. LEFT: This modest façade, with its front-gabled sloping roof line, provides the appropriate massing for an ashlar stone application. TOP: River Rock as an agreeable counterpoint to lap and shingle siding.

LEFT: Hidden by trees, this stone-clad porte cochère invites visitors to recall celebrated building techniques and masonry craftsmanship. TOP: The characteristic randomness of a rubble stone fortifies the physique of this home.

TOP: *Simple forms and a modest application of stone regards a revered finishing touch that includes brick and distressed stucco. RIGHT: This house's signature statement — its main tower — is wrapped with a generous amount of rough-faced rubble. Brick columns provide a nice counterpoint to the stone.*

This home in Idaho showcases rough hewn and rubble-
like stone with a darker color palette indicative of the
geology of the region.

Just as important as the welcoming gesture of an open gate or the bravura of a paneled entrance door, stone embraces and safeguards both resident and visitor.

ABOVE and OPPOSITE PAGE: Combining brick and
stone can create remarkable rhythms and intriguing
harmonies. RIGHT: Colored mortar similar to the value
of the stone softens a large expanse.

As the sun begins its descent to dusk, the mood changes as shadows lengthen. It is remarkable to note how much the stone's color palette changes throughout the day.

TOP: A stone–clad load bearing wall underneath a second storey porch visually supports both vertical and horizontal planes. RIGHT: The darker colored grout and expressed joint contrasts with the lighter color tones of the stone.

Stone relegates itself to a supporting role in favor of
other stylings. LEFT: The tiled risers of this exterior patio
stairway are a respectful homage to early 20th century
California potteries. TOP: A simple garden wall creates
a pedestal for desert plants.

Whether public or private, outdoor gathering spaces shaped by stone become a relaxing retreat from the activities of a hectic day. And it is stone, unlike other building materials, that can create a warm, textural and colorful embrace.

The rhythm of fire and the dance of the flame. Don't you always find yourself lost in thought when you gaze into fire? A relationship with fire is everlasting. The same is true with stone. They are both respectful family members at a natural gathering...the stone fireplace. So, enjoy the following pages of exterior fireplaces. They showcase just how intimate that relationship is.

TOP: *Modernist stone columns, with ledgestones installed as a dry stack, stand as sentries for an outdoor pool and patio.*
RIGHT: *This fieldstone, generally wider than it is tall, also demonstrates its appeal when installed as a dry-stack.*

Expansive arched porte cochères adorned with a
monochromatic dry-stacked ledgestone transitions
outdoors and indoors.

The muted tones of this dry-stacked ledgestone
complements the tropical architectural style. UPPER
LEFT and ABOVE: A feeling of transcendence envelops.
Tranquil and languid. LOWER LEFT: The ocean blue
window glass. The bleached white walls and cantilevered
balcony forms. The contrasting texture of the stone wall.
The sum of all parts that comprise a whole.

When stacked, the smooth, water–worn texture of beach
stones form a surprisingly trim and tidy assemblage for
installations more modest in appearance.

RIGHT: Grout, when applied liberally — and with an artist's flair — can create an Old-World appearance. TOP: Water and Stone. Two interconnected elements perfectly suited to complement outdoor jacuzzis. LEFT: The ashlar cut of smoother-faced stones neatly dresses this elevated pool and patio spa.

LEFT: *Doors wide open, this stone barn-like structure greets visitors in a well-dressed manner.* ABOVE: *This Juliet balcony, cantilevered from the face of a heavily textured stone wall, is an intimate extension of the interior room.*

The referenced Italianate architectural style of this home
encourages this installation of rectilinear-shaped stone.
TOP: The low-pitched roof, overhanging eaves and
decorative brackets achieve visual prominence above the
stone. *RIGHT:* The massive stone façade is softened by
the smooth texture of the accents.

In daylight, the same stone house (from the previous page)
appears dramatically different. The light of the day warms up
the tonality of the stone. Architecturally, the building forms
seem appropriately massed with just the right amount of stone.

REVIVING INDIGENOUS STYLES

"Each material speaks a language of its own."

– Frank Lloyd Wright

Stone has a particularly rich visual vocabulary. At different times, stone says different things. In the rosy light of early morning it tends to whisper. In the late afternoon, stone often speaks with a golden tongue. Architectural design is, to some extent, the process of looking for the new — new designs and new building materials. But it also is a process of looking back. Preserving the things that, for good reason, have endured.

As an example, ashlar-cut profiles capture the precision stonework of late 19th century brownstone townhomes in New York City. Rustic designs with fieldstone pay homage to rural areas of Europe. Adobe profiles preserve the look and feel of traditional buildings from the southwestern United States. In each instance, Eldorado Stone is committed to ensuring that the architectural styles that spoke to our great-grandparents — in the Old World and the New — will be heard by future generations.

ABOVE: The massing of overgrouted stone forms. Deep, recessed windows accentuate the bulbous shafts of the patio's baluster columns. The oversized chimney hood. All visual indications of the influence of Old-World styles.

ODE TO TUSCANY

The stone. The amber hills bejeweled with cypress. The scent of ripening olives and grapes. The distant echoes of the Renaissance. Tuscany speaks to you. And even if you don't know Italian, somehow you understand.

As the birthplace of Michelangelo, Leonardo Da Vinci and Brunelleschi, Italy is understandably proud of its artistic and architectural heritage. An architectural heritage immensely popular worldwide. This love affair with Italy — and Tuscany especially — continues to inspire designers who covet Old-World styles from Romanesque to Neo-Classical.

Accurately capturing the details of Old-World styles requires equal parts understanding and vision. The selection of stone shapes, textures and color palettes, and the refinement of the final details, are all equivalent partners in the journey.

A closer look at the images on the following pages reveals a reverence for the vernacular of Tuscan and Old-World style. And incredible as it may seem, this is a style re-created not in Florence, Siena, or Pisa, but in the United States, with Eldorado Stone's architectural stone and brick veneers.

The choice of grout has an enormous impact on the final look of a stone installation. Many installations that mimic an Old-World style are overgrouted where mortar intentionally overlaps the face of the brick and stone, widening joints and producing an irregular, rustic look.

Historic renovations and re-creations always seem to benefit from a generous amount of stone. And the more irregularly-shaped the better.

TOP: The modest stylings of this antique writing table and Louis XIV chair accessorizes the adjoining brick wall. RIGHT: Elongated rough-faced brick and contrasting mortar joints. Heavy wooden beams and a rusty bell. It really is a chunk of history.

BRICK: A HISTORIC IMPRESSION

Brick isn't just a great building material, it's a chunk of history. It's one of the world's oldest building materials. Some samples from the Middle East date back to 7500 B.C. Just hold a piece of worn brick in your hand and wonder: Is that hint of amber from an old copper mine? Were those edges worn by wind whipping through the Appalachians? Was that interesting fissure caused by a driving rain off the Baltic — or a 12th-century archer's arrow?

Eldorado Brick was molded from century-old buildings throughout Europe. Each brick unique. Full of character, story and admirable imperfection.

And now a toast: Here's to brick in the kitchen. Brick on the patio. Brick in the family room. Brick in a cozy wine cellar. A wine cellar from which, incidentally, your friends and family will never want to leave.

Antebellum influences and details embrace this classic
southern home. Brick adorns its ground floor and a private
courtyard welcomes you with classic southern hospitality.

STANDARD OR RAKED JOINT

A joiner or blunt masonry instrument is used to create a concave, raked out look in the mortar.

FULL JOINT

A full joint is similar to a standard joint however, the grout level is almost flush with the face of the brick.

OVERGROUT JOINT

The mortar overlaps the face of the brick, widening joints and producing an irregular, rustic look.

WEEP OR OOZE JOINT

The grout oozes out of the joints to appear as though the weight of the bricks above has forced out the excess grout.

BEAD JOINT

The grout extrudes beyond the brick face but it's cleaner looking and a more purposeful technique than a weep joint.

GRAPEVINE JOINT

Dragging a thin, blunt instrument along the middle of the wet grout scores the grout leaving a thin visible scar.

No matter how beautiful the brick is, the grout technique — and how well it is executed — is as important as the brick itself. To a remarkable degree an impressive grout technique, both in color hue and finished joint methods, significantly enhances the beauty and believability of all installations. Brick patterns, grout color and joint techniques should be researched and discussed prior to installation. The many techniques employed by masonry craftsmen greatly affects the final appearance.

LEFT: The dentil band of brick installed underneath the eave is angled to create a detail not commonly seen. TOP: Installed, the warmer tone of this brick veneer and the contrasting warm gray colored grout is an appealing combination that accentuates the rustic beauty of each component.

TOP: *The modernity of this urban loft space and the contrasting earnestness of the brick's running bond installation pattern creates quite a pairing.* RIGHT: *Rough-faced brick flows effortlessly from one wall face to another.*

This Southwest-styled home demonstrates its architectural reverence to adobe with a deeply recessed entrance, tiled second storey exterior staircase and thick wooden lintels.

ADOBE: SIMPLE, HONEST, ENDURING

Adobe has been a popular building material for thousands of years. Cultures as diverse as the Egyptians, the Chinese and the Anasazi have built remarkable structures with sundried earth mixed with other materials such as sand and straw.

For such a simple material, adobe can evoke surprisingly rich, complex architectural moods. If you've ever had the pleasure of entering a traditional adobe structure, you probably remember the experience. Many adobe buildings project a powerful sense of solidity and permanence that resonates long after you've walked away.

Look closely at the photograph of the interior living room where adobe is used masterfully to help bring bright outdoor light inside. At first glance, the walls simply look pale. But as you look more closely, the texture of the adobe starts to emerge, as do subtle and surprisingly warm tones. The living room practically glows with the rose tones of sunrise. Finally, notice how the adobe, through striking contrast of light and dark, brings out the best in the wood furniture, the ceiling beams and the dark iron sconces.

Working closely with architects and preservationists, Eldorado Stone has developed an array of adobe profiles that capture the essence of this revered building material. For designers seeking the authentic feel of the Southwest, Eldorado Adobe can be an outstanding option.

Construction of Egyptian pyramids
completed with adobe bricks

2500 BC

Adobe bricks used to help
fortify the Great Wall of China

700–300 BC

Building begins on the Taos Pueblo
adobe village in New Mexico

1500 AD

| 2000 BC | 1000 BC | 0 | 1000 AD | 2000 AD |

1300–400 BC

Tres Zapotes, an Olmec site in
Mexico, is the first adobe-brick
pyramid site in Mesoamerica

450 AD

The eighth stage of the
Huaca del Sol is completed in
Peru, containing an estimated
140 million adobe bricks

1769–1823 AD

Spanish missionaries use adobe
to build a total of 21 missions
along the California coast

GEORGIAN

AMERICAN HOUSE STYLES

Early stone structures in the United States benefited from the skilled stone workers who immigrated here, particularly from Scotland, Germany, Italy, and the Scandinavian countries. Throughout the country the abundance of regional stone types became the foundation — both literally and figuratively — for classic American Homes.

Limestone and rubble in the Northeast. Bluestone in Pennsylvania. Ledgestones in the Carolinas. Sandstone in Western United States. Add to that, brick, adobe and other earthen materials and it's easy to understand why these building materials remain a dramatic expression for anyone contemplating designing, building or living their dream.

The American house styles illustrated on these pages don't represent a comprehensive list. It is, simply, a broad sampling of styles built throughout the states. Styles that benefited from an abundance of stone. From early 17th and 18th century Georgian, Colonial and Federal styles symmetrically ordered and gracefully detailed to simplified Farmhouses both European influenced and modestly Western. Stone types selected for specific styles remain esteemed depictions for that particular architectural statement. Even squat, linear Prairie style homes and Craftsman bungalows conjure images of particular stone types appropriate for their form.

These American House styles are a foretaste for the images following. Structures that present iconic interpretations of form, texture and visual color in concert with their heritage.

WESTERN FARMHOUSE

CONTEMPORARY

PRAIRIE

EUROPEAN FARMHOUSE

CRAFTSMAN

LEFT: This home appears to take its cue from Victorian Queen Anne architecture with a style neither orderly or easy to define. Turrets, porches, brackets and bay windows combine with stone and shingle siding in unexpected ways. TOP: The chill of winter is no match for the stone-clad façade of this farmhouse style home.

*The Prairie style roof line of this home caps the majesty
of the dominant stone columns on the front façade.*

TOP: The humble architecture of this southern-styled residence makes brick an obvious choice for its ground floor façade. RIGHT: The color of the installed rustic ledgestone balances the palette of the roofing shingles and accent colors on this farmhouse style home.

INTERIORS

" *The finest workers in stone are not copper or steel tools, but the gentle touches of air and water working at their leisure with a liberal allowance of time.*"

–Henry David Thoreau

With its dazzling array of tones, textures and shapes, stone is an incredibly expressive building material. Increasingly, among enlightened architects and builders, the use of stone isn't limited to exteriors and façades. More and more, stone is finding its way inside homes.

Stone brings warmth and character to stainless-steel laden kitchens. It introduces subtle color to libraries, dens, and bedrooms. Today, stone graces family rooms and libraries on the East Coast, greatrooms and master suites of the South and interior courtyards with fireplaces in the West.

Prepare to be dazzled by the living room on page 134 where a fieldledge fireplace, resplendent with warm grays and soft ambers, serves as the perfect counterpoint to the floor-to-ceiling view out into the wilderness. What gourmet aspiring chef wouldn't love the kitchens on page 122, 124 and 136? We'll leave the bedroom scene on page 141— with the Mesquite Cliffstone fireplace — to your imagination.

TOP: Irregularly-shaped stone with a liberal wash of colored grout over the entire face of the stone calms the usually strident appearance. RIGHT: Often thought of as cold and austere, stone can actually transform to warm and inviting.

The vineyard, often characterized loosely by the French term "terroir", or "sense of place", refers to the grapevine's geology and geography. FAR LEFT: So, is it possible, that much of the flavor of the well-appointed wine vault could be imparted in the wine? A simple taste may tell. ABOVE and LEFT: If it is true, that wine improves with age, couldn't the same be said of a stone wine vault? And what better pairing than these two revered and historic participants?

TOP: *A stone-clad alcove surrounds the interior living room fireplace.* RIGHT: *A festive cheer fills the room with cherished memories of holidays past and present.*

When the kitchen is the focal point, stone dresses the
area wonderfully. LEFT: Stone is installed on the
stove's ventilation hood and the surface surrounding
the small clerestory windows. TOP: The horizontal and
vertical informality of the stacked stone complements the
traditional design of this kitchen and its components.

The notion of a soaking tub becomes increasingly appealing within the context of primal elements. LEFT: Stone wall, bath and fireplace create a luxurious end-of-day diversion. TOP: Eastern intuition considers placement and arrangement a vital aesthetic of the built environment. And, simplicity, the true nature of direct individual experience.

TOP: *The stone fireplace ablaze. The log cabin in the mountains. As warm and cozy inside as it is bracing and blustery outside. RIGHT: Historically, farmhouses had a back-entranced room where muddy boots and clothing could be shed before entering the main house. This mudroom, and its dry-stacked stone wall, transitions outdoor to indoor.*

TOP: Nighttime falls. Brick columns and a colossal stone wall await the guests soon to arrive. RIGHT: The formality of traditional interior decor is functional, uncomplicated and relaxed. Often, the stone fireplace is the centerpiece.

LEFT: A stone wall in a backup role where kitchen island counters and tables take center stage. TOP: A heavy wooden beam over the stovetop visually supports the darker hues of the overgrouted stone wall and rich palette of this kitchen design.

LEFT: This grand interior, with its modernist hints of simplification and absence of ornament, creates a statement bold enough to welcome large stone columns. ABOVE: In contrast, this southwestern bedroom's focal point is its native American influenced barrel-shaped fireplace.

CREATING
AUTHENTICITY

*" The noblest pleasure is the joy
of understanding."*

–Leonardo da Vinci

Creating authenticity, with respect for building styles and architectural flair, involves a keen eye and an educated approach. It's the perfect combination of vision, form, style and craftsmanship. An orchestrated approach that can be easily attained given the right tools. Tools that the owner, architect, designer, builder and mason use to create enchanting places and exquisite spaces. Spaces all the more beautiful when adorned with stone.

Creating authenticity and believability involves more than simply "sticking" the stone on a wall. Selecting the appropriate stone type and grout technique greatly affects the visual impact. Finishing touches often include the addition of corners, accents and accessories.

The information on the following pages can be used as a reference when discussing the many aspects of installed stone veneer. Though not comprehensive, it does provide a starting point. Eldorado encourages you to explore, research and educate yourself so you'll appreciate the craftsmanship of a truly believable architectural stone veneer installation.

STONE STYLES

Eldorado Stone's manufactured stone veneer profiles are cast from molds made from natural stone. Stones that are used to create the most authentic and most believable architectural stone veneer. The broad categories and profile names available from Eldorado Stone are loosely categorized by the geological classification they descended from.

Stone identification is often a mix of the scientific identification of the geology of rocks and the artistic description that relates to the stone's appearance. But whatever the name, stone can be cut, dressed, installed and finished in different fashions. It has been this way for eons and continues to be relevant when installing Eldorado Stone.

The images below do not represent the entire geological spectrum of stone, rock and minerals. They do help in the understanding and articulation of stone types desired for a particular project.

ASHLAR   RIVER ROCK   HILLSTONE

LEDGESTONE   RUBBLE   LEDGESTONE WITH RUBBLE

THE IMPACT OF GROUT

Considering how many centuries masons have faced the jigsaw puzzle of stonework, it's no surprise that there are many different grout techniques. Naturally, the color of the grout, whether it complements or contrasts with the stone, has an enormous impact on the final effect. Three of the most enduring grout techniques are the standard joint, the dry-stack joint and the overgrout joint. The standard (raked) joint is achieved by laying stones approximately a finger-width apart. Before it hardens, the mortar is raked with a tool to achieve consistent depth. As the name suggests, a dry-stack technique eliminates the use of visible mortar between stones. The effect produces very tightly stacked stones. With overgrout — sometimes called a "sack finish"— masons traditionally use burlap sacks to smooth the mortar so it overlaps the face of the stone. It's an increasingly popular option that creates irregular joints that look and feel like Old-World craftsmanship.

OPPOSITE PAGE: This combined stone and brick installation is finished with an overgrout technique to create the classic Old-World look.

WARM COLORED GROUT

This brick was installed using a warmer colored grout with an overgrout joint. Compared to the cooler gray grout used (below) this particular grout color decreases the contrast of warmer tones in the brick.

COOL COLORED GROUT

A standard gray grout was used in this installation. The grout affects perception of the brick's color after installation. Cooler colored grout contrasts with the warmer tones of the brick.

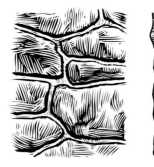

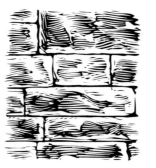

Standard Joint　　　　　*Dry-Stack Joint*　　　　　*Overgrout Joint*

ABOVE: The recessed window allows the corner pieces of this adobe veneer to mimic a thick, natural adobe wall. ABOVE RIGHT: Archstone corners add a refinement and necessary thickness over the arched garage door.

LEFT: Thick, ashlar-cut wall caps rest assuredly atop this exterior wall. ABOVE: A harmonious mix of stone and brick with matching wall and column caps creates detailed authenticity.

FINISHING TOUCHES

Authentic installations with stone veneer include a number of refined details that combine to create the desired beauty. The balance of components such as wood, metal, glass, paint, furniture and landscaping greatly affects the overall feeling and appearance of a space adorned with stone.

In addition to building materials, an understanding of suitable stone details and accents will complete the overall look. During installation, a talented mason will select stones to create a unique pattern of shape, size, color and thickness. Also, a generous use of stone veneer corners for perpendicular wall-to-wall transitions will produce the appearance of a full-sized natural stone installation. Finalizing your project with accessory accents such as lintels, archstones, window quoins, wall caps and other finishing elements offers functionality with a decorative finish.

The journey from vision to completion can be a very rewarding experience. Combined elements working together harmoniously create memorable spaces bursting with texture, warmth, color and permanence. Permanence that is alluring.

PROFILE & GROUT INDEX

INTERIORS

CREATING AUTHENTICITY

A visual representation of the basic grout techniques in this book:

Standard grout technique

Dry-Stack technique

Overgrout technique

CREDITS

PHOTOGRAPHERS

Alain Jaramillo Photography: 109. **Dino Tonn Photography:** 35, 141.
Eric Figge Photography, Inc.: 02, 08, 10, 28, 29, 64, 65, 66, 67, 77, 122, 136,
137. **InSite Architectural Photography:** 60 top. **Jeremy Hess Photography:**
18, 19, 100, 103. **John Bare Photography:** 15, 21, 22, 23, 24, 25 top, 25
bottom, 32, 33, 34, 36, 37, 38 top, 38 bottom, 46, 47 top, 54, 55, 60 bottom, 61,
62, 63, 68, 69, 74, 78 top, 80, 81, 93, 104, 113, 118, 121, 132, 145, 150, 151 top
right. **John Bare / Design Lens:** 30 top, 30 bottom. **Linna Photographics:** 47
bottom, 49, 102, 106, 107, 119 top, 120, 126, 130, 131, 133, 139, 140.
Owen McGoldrick Photography: 43, 76, 78, 79, 83, 110, 142, 149, 151 bottom
left. **Peter Christiansen Valli Photographic Services:** 26, 44. **Reimers & Hollar
Photographers:** 56, 58, 59, 84, 89, 91, 94, 95, 96, 97, 123, 138, 148, 151 top left.
Roharik Photographic: 16. **The Shadowlight Group:** 82, 92, 124.
Courtesy of Coastal Living Magazine: 86, 87, 108. **Courtesy of Southern
Accents Magazine:** 119 bottom. **Thomas J. Story / Courtesy of Sunset
Magazine:** 129.

ARCHITECTS / DESIGNERS

Ann Matteson, Ann Matteson Consulting: 38 top. **Athens Design Group:**
54, 55, 109, 145. **Architects Northwest:** 47 bottom, 120. **Bassenian Lagoni
Architects:** cover, 08, 21, 28, 29, 64, 65, 66, 67, 77, 122, 137. **Curtis Gelotte
Architects:** 49, 107, 140. **Edmonds International:** 52, 53. **HKS Hill Glazier
Studio:** 54, 55, 109, 145. **Design by Kim Stits California Colors:** 56, 58, 59,
76, 78 bottom, 79, 149, 151 bottom. **Knitter & Associates:** 62, 93. **Design by:
Leslie Cohen Design:** 123. **MAI Design Group, Marsh & Associates, Inc.:** 15,
22, 25, 74. **Murphy & Associates:** 119 top. **Scheurer Architects, Inc.:** 02, 10,
15, 20, 23, 37, 38 top, 46, 50, 51, 63, 90, 94, 95, 96, 97, 104, 113, 114, 115, 118,
121, 132, 136, 151 top right, 151 top left. **Tim Schulze:** 76, 78 bottom, 79, 149,
151 bottom.

BUILDERS / DEVELOPERS

ALHEL Grupo Inmobiliario: 52, 53. **Baywood Development:** 02, 10, 32,
33, 36. **Brookfield Homes:** 63, 104, 151 top. **Christopher Homes:** 50, 51.
Columbia Builders: 100, 103. **Columbia Homes:** 19. **Exceptional Homes
by Andre:** 134. **Fazzolari Custom Homes:** 126, 133. **Greystone Homes:** 08,
21, 28, 29, 77, 122, 137. **Insite Homes:** 119 top. **Keller Homes:** 38 top. **Laing
Luxury Sentinels:** 30 top, 30 bottom. **Lennar Communities:** 15, 22, 74, 80.
London Bay Homes: 90. **MacPherson Construction:** 49, 107, 140.
Par Development: 48. **Pardee Homes:** 60 top, 94, 95, 96, 97. **Parmenter
Homes:** 47 bottom, 102, 120, 130. **Pinn Bros. Fine Homes:** 62, 93. **Stafford
Homes:** 17. **StoneRidge Custom Homes, Inc.:** 139. **Taurus Homes:** 131.
WCI Communities, Inc.: 68, 69, 78 top.

PROJECTS

Bahlay, Acapulco: 52, 53. **BlackRock Country Club and Community, ID:**
24, 25 Top and Bottom. **The Bridges at Rancho Santa Fe, CA:** 15, 22, 74, 80.
Builder Magazine's Show Home 2003, NV (Southern Highlands, Enclave): 23,
46, 113, 118, 121, 132. **Coastal Living Idea House 2007; Bon Secour Village,
AL:** 86, 87, 108. **La Bellezza at Peregrine, CO:** 38 top. **The Montage Spa and
Resort, CA:** 54, 55, 145. **The Parkland Golf and Country Club and Community,
FL:** 68, 69, 78 top. **Southern Accents Showhouse 2007, Homestead Preserve;
Hot Springs, VA:** 119 bottom. **Sunset Idea House 2004; Valencia, CA:** 47 top,
60 bottom. **Sunset Idea House 2004; Verado, AZ:** 37. **Sunset Idea House 2007;
Tahoe(Truckee), CA:** 129.

*Eldorado Stone extends its sincere gratitude to the many architects, builders, developers,
designers, masons, and homeowners who have not been specifically credited in this
book. They too are trustworthy partners whose imagination and expertise are ultimately
accountable for Eldorado's success as manufacturers of The Most Believable
Architectural Stone Veneer in the World.*™